This book belongs to:

_____

ISBN-13: 978-0-578-50139-0
K 4 Books Publishing, LLC

THE PERFECT PAIR

Written by
KAYA

Illustrated by CORLETTE DOUGLAS
Art Direction & Design by SHIBAZZLE

She plays dress up & sips tea like the Queen

She does cartwheels
in her favorite
ripped jeans

She keeps everything neat and tidy

She shakes things up
like every day
is Friday!

She likes pink tutus
and fancy shiny pearls

She likes sporty shoes
and colorful swirls

She sits quietly
with books to read

She reads upside down
while swinging on a tree

She likes to prance
She likes to dance

Big curly 'fros
Pigtails and bows

Dresses that flow
Sparkle that shows
Sneakers that glow
Slime that grows

A love that shows
A bond that grows

Math problems that only she knows
Goggles, lab coats and erupting volcanoes!

Stories to debate
Memories to create

Space to sleep
Secrets to keep

Jewelry to spare
Things to share

Burdens to bear
Sisters who care

KAYA

♥ Kaya's love of writing began with a secret childhood poetry journal and continued to flourish at age 11 after becoming the youngest semi-finalist on record at the Library of Congress's Annual Poetry Contest. From that moment on, Kaya knew she would no longer keep her poetry hidden but continue to share her love of writing with the world, one story at a time.

Now, Kaya, is a proud mom of four, entrepreneur, and author, giving you a glimpse inside the colorful world of sisterhood with the release of her first poetry book, The Perfect Pair! The inspirations behind this charming story are two beautiful souls, her daughters, Kira and Kori -- two rare gems who are radiant lights to everyone around them.

CORLETTE DOUGLAS

Corlette Douglas is an illustrator
and designer born and raised in the
heart of Brooklyn. Best known
for working in watercolors, gouache
and colored pencils, Corlette creates colorful,
whimsical, childlike worlds
for all to enjoy.

SHIBAZZLE

SHIBAZZLE LLC is a NYC-based visual media
& design house focused on creating high quality
work with uniqueness, intelligence and a splash
of spunk. Creative director Kelly Jones is a veteran
storyboard artist & designer with over a decade
of experience in the graphic design
and animation industries.

SPECIAL THANKS

First, I would like to acknowledge Christ
who is the center of my life and my foundation.

To my children:
Kira, Kyle, Kori & Khye (also known as The K's).
Thank you all for inspiring me to consider
the impossible, for challenging me to push past boundaries
and for being exactly what I needed in order to grow.
Your support gives me strength and your love will continue
to write the story of my heart forever.
I love you!

CPSIA information can be obtained at www.ICGtesting.com
Printed in the USA
LVIW012223190919
631219LV00051B/811